Life , A blend of Agony and Pride

Dr Ritu Sharma

Presentation by *BookLeaf Publishing*

Web: www.bookleafpub.com

E-mail: info@bookleafpub.com

ISBN:9789360949136

First edition 2024

DEDICATION

My Mati (Dr Ramola Masand Manucha)

Ex Capt AMC

My Chote (Dr Varsha Manucha Anand)

My lifelines

Adu, Sharvi, Vahitu, Ariya

Upasna, Tripti, Manmeet—thank you for being my pillars.

ACKNOWLEDGEMENT

I bow to all who till date make me believe I am a miracle, with their patient listening, their presence, their holding onto my chaos, by being there for me unconditionally.

PREFACE

My soul is the ink to my pen as I put words to paper that have and are a journey of sorts sketching me who I am, as ME, as Ritu, everyday.

Table of Contents

Mati

This one—for Mati

Today I sat thinking about her,
I think about her all the time,
But that is only thinking about her,
Today was different,
It was a visual of screenshots of her life,
That which I would set aside every time and
always.

Wonder why today I let them be screened loud
and clear till my memory zone was all of hers.

The 5th in 12 siblings,
She is younger to 4 and elder to 7,
The younger ones grew up in her lap,
I did not make her a mother,
She has been a mother to all 7 of them long
years now,

79 to be exact.

She studied medicine and to share the burden of
her elders dumped higher studies,
She joined the Army,
The first batch of lady officers,
The year was 65,
The salary she earned was saved,
So, no living life to the fullest,
Life had to wait to be lived by her.

She met my dad,
Her prince charming,
A Soldier like her,
They got married,
And then came 3 of us,
She yet again asked life to wait,
She dumped her career in the Army midway for
us and for her Soldier,
No pension, nothing came home barring the
uniform and memories.

As we starting growing up,
Her focus was our future,
Her focus was her Soldiers... soldering,
And, yet again,
She asked life to wait to be lived by her,
Yet again she asked moments to wait,
Till they could be only hers,

She moulded her taste buds to fit into her
Soldiers and then ours too.

She kept moving,
Staying the way her Soldier made her,
Working if she could,
A doctor by profession,
And she has worked all 50 years as a medico,
But nothing adding to her profile,
Big salary packages,
Senior appointments,
A name for herself,
Nothing at all,
I forget how many places she rendered herself
completely to as a medico,
The priority forever remained her Soldier and
us.

Today as the screenshots of life as lived by her
whizzed past my zone,
I saw a vague shadow standing still at one
place,
The visuals kept moving,
That shadow did not budge,
That is when I tried to knock the shadow down,
Trying to erase it,
The shadow was blocking the screening,
And, then,
That shadow turned back to me,

And said
"I am not going anywhere,
I am life,
I am moments,
I envelope every bit, every piece of what Ramola
is,
Every bit of what makes Ramola the woman she
is,
Ramola has been shunning me away for years
now,
And I have been waiting for her to open this
envelope,
That will truly unfold Ramola to meet herself,
But she has still kept me on a hold,
81 years is a long time,
I am life,
I can't wait forever."

And then I changed the visuals,
I wanted to understand which was this Ramola,
The Ramola I knew nothing about,
And that is when,
I saw a lot of Ramola dumped everywhere in
closets,
The closets locked and the keys kept away by
her.

I asked her for the keys to the closet,
She smiled at me saying it is too late now,

She had lost track,
She did not remember where she had kept the
keys,
She had no track of what she would want to do
to be Ramola again,
She said her taste buds don't understand A la
carte anymore,
She told me,
To let be,
She asked me to ask that shadow to go away,
And to not wait anymore,
She wasn't the same Ramola anymore,
She was now so much of our Mati,
So much of her Soldier's wife,
So much of so many relationships,
That it would take her a whole lifetime to
remember why Ramola had asked time to wait.

It took me 5 decades to realize Ramola had lost
herself somewhere,
And Ramola,
Ramola doesn't even realize that she has lost
herself somewhere.

She feels so complete in being what
relationships have made of her.

There is only one thing she remembers,

There is only one thing—she is happy living as
Ramola everytime she can,
There is only one moment that Ramola cherishes
with PRIDE,
And that wearing her name plate which reads,
Capt Ramola Masand Manucha,
The only one moment she refuses to let go,
And that is when she can flaunt being a Soldier,
And she does that with amazing grace,
For her,
Every moment relived as Capt Ramola Masand
Manucha,
Is a complete life lived as Ramola,
She seeks nothing else,
My Mati

Ritu
D/O Capt Ramola Masand Manucha

Sad Prose

Sad prose runs through my veins,
Feelings are for me distorted,
My vision is blurred,
My soul still breathes, sipping from years of
undaunting love and affections from strangers
who are now more than family.

Cracks, unlocked doors, gaps in the window
shields, incomplete sentences I leave behind,
forgive me for these errors, and fill them up with
your authentication of memories.

Life does go on

But the remains, the captures, the bits and pieces
of you in me and me in you matter and that is
what gives meaning to our lives, that is what
keeps us enveloped safely, that is what will torch
the paths ahead for me

*You all rock like a bundle of joy, like that tree
that stands forever irrespective of the sun, the
rain, the thunder, the storms.
You never let bad weather wither me, your
presence still holds onto the ship and we
smoothly keep sailing,
Whenever we meet*

*We came, we went, we will keep coming and
going, but the US will remain forever deeply
engraved as a part of my humble being, as a
part of my life forever*

*Loads and loads of love and hugs to all who
make my family complete.*

Kitnee Ritu See Hone Lagee Hoon Main

Thodee bikhree see main,
Thodee naraz see main,
Thodee befhikree see main,
Thodee khudh see main,
Apne man kee karne lagee hoon ab main,
Thoda thoda khud ke liye jeene lagee hoon main,
Sooraj kee kirne,
Chanda kee chandni,
Badalon kee baarish,
Hawa ke jhonke,
Bagon main jhoole,
In sab se ab milne lagee hoon main.

Bewajhe yunhee muskuratee hoon ab main,
Mayusee ko masayel banatee nahee ab main,
Yeh jhalka ansoon kabhee,

Woh ayee hansee abhee,
Aina mera dost kabhee,
Aine se sharmayee kabhee main,
Kitnee RITU see hone lagee hoon main.

Main 🖤🖤🖤🖤 *Ritu* 🖤🖤

Karva ka Chand

She celebrates the love in her
One reason more for her to feel celebrated
All the fantasizing of
Red and the green and the yellow
All the hue and cry of what to wear
Of what to adorn
Of what to drape
Of which design of colors of orange embellish
her palms
Of how and when and where to stand and pose

Oh my my
She is all about a dream today
Let the number of years be
She is just She
She is the beautiful woman in love

Don't tie her with superstition
Let her spread her wings lavishly
Let her paint herself in her choices of colors
Let her drown in her love for herself
The more She falls in love with who she becomes
with serenity, with peace, with smiles
The more She will love you with that freedom of
being all yours

It is truly her day
Let her be the reason you are
And see the magic of love
Unconditional love

And not to forget
The moon
The moon is her first love tonight 🤍🤍🤍

Ritu 🥰

Kaalee Ghanee Raat

Kaalee ghanee raat,
Dhalte dhalte,
Sooraj ka jharonka khol jatee hai,
Roz roz,
Har baar,

Aur, phir, kaee baar,
Kabhee kabhee,
Roz roz,
Mujhe sooraj badlon ke anchal main chup ke
aankh micholee karta dikhta hai.

Dhoondh rahee hoon apna woh aasman,
Jane kab se,
Jab sooraj kee kirne,
Bina kisee parde main chup ke,
Mujhe apnee chamak se,

Bhigo jayengee,

Tab, shayad, samajh paungee,
Kaalee raat, sunharee subah ka andesha hotee
hai

To Let Go

To Let Go

Is it all about
To just let go
And to let go of what
Let go of
Relationships
Let go of
Emotions
Let go of
Bonds
Let go of
What you build around you
Let go of
What you earn as experience, as respect,
Let go of

What made you to be the person you are
Let go of
Scars of battles won and lost and learned from
Let go of
Memories
Or
Let go of
The closet of memories
Let go of
Smiles that were
Tears that helped you see through that mirage of
the unknown as they wiped away the frost on the
eyelids
Let go of what?

These are earnings of a lifetime,
A lifetime, irrespective of the time, as it is for
each one of us,

How then let go of earnings of a life?
Won't it be like keeping the safe open?
Waiting for someone to rob us off?

Yes, that's what it explains itself as in the two
words,
Let go

I am contemplating,
I'm trying to rephrase the jest here,

It has to be something else,
Of what they mean,
When they say,
Let go

Because I don't want to be robbed off,
So, can't let go

Let's rephrase

Ritu

Rishtey ... Relationships

Kabhee ulhje uljhe se yeh rishtey,
Kabhee suljhe suljhe se yeh rishtey,

Time can never be the reason for them,
Time cannot measure their depth,
Relationships are not dates or weeks or months
or years on the calendar,
Relationships are simply, purely, serenely,
majestically just relationships.

Roz roz ek naya safar tay karte hain yeh rishtey,
Har pal main zindagi ko naye moh ke dhagon
main bun dete hain yeh rishtey,
Phir unhee palon ko ruhanee mazbootee se
roshan bhee kar dete hain yeh rishtey.

They are bonds for a life,
At the same time they set us free for a life,
They tie us in feelings of the soul with colours of
spirituality,
And then they give our soul wings to connect
with our dreams

Kabhee hum unhe peeche chod aate hain,
Usee dam woh saath saath chalte bhee rahte
hain,
Juda sa ho jate hain hum unse kabhee kabhee,
Mutasir bhee hote hain har pal unse hum,
Kumhar kee dhanee kee kachee mitee se yeh
rishtey,
Ek naya roop har pal lete hain,
Mayus karte nahee mujhe kabhee,
Kab, kahan, kyun, kaise, sawalon kee hathkadee
se baandhte nahee mujhe.

I never have to go looking for them,
They don't have to come looking for me,
They are the true meaning of spiritual bonding,
Thay are me all the time,
I am them all the time,
Relationships.

Kisee shart ke mohtaj nahee yeh rishtey,
They weave the threads of life together,

Adding beauty to moments lived,
Samay ke kanton tak simet ke reh jayain,
Aise nazuk nahee yeh rishtey,
Aur yehee to inkee azmat hai,

Badlte rehna inkee taseer hai mere dost,
Mere har roop, har rang, har jazbat ko ek naya
naam dete hain yeh roz roz,

Inhee se shikayat,
Inhee se shikwa,
Yeh roothte bhee hain,
Yeh mana bhee lete hain,
Rangon ke is jahan main,
Mausekee inhee se hai,
Yeh rishtey.

Relationships .....
They make me who I am.

Juda yeh rishtey kabhee nahee hote mujhse,
Inke ehsas kee dor meree ruh ko shakhsiyat
detee hai,
Mujhe nihar dete hain,
Yeh rishtey 

Ritu

Jo Guzar Gaye Woh Raste

Samne aane wale raste
Kitne hee roshan kyun na hoon,
Samne aane wala sheher kitna hee pasandida
kyun na hoon,
Nayee mulakatain kitnee bhee khushnuma kyun
na hon,
Nayee yaareeyon kee chehek kitna bhee apne
paas kyun na bulayen,

Jo guzar gaye woh raste,
Jise chod chale woh sheher,
Woh sham dhale milna milana,
Woh yareeyan jinki reh guzar humaree ruh thee,

Humko kuch adhoora sa chod jate hain,
Chalte hum jate hain,
Par woh yadain,
Woh rahain,
Woh dost,
Woh tum,
Woh hum,
Kuch khalee pan to kasakta hai,
Aur kuch apne ko bhee to unhee wadiyon main
bekhayalee main chod aate hain hum.

Fly Away

My daughters

Adu, Sharvi, Vahitu

They have made of themselves who they are,
We were just the shelter.

They walked the path on their own,
Learning, falling, exploring,
Their likes, their dislikes,
Their favorites are genuinely theirs,
They have earned the privilege to be proud of
who they are and will become,
And we call them our pride,
In fact, they made us into who we are,

They added to our incomplete marinations a
dash of humbleness, humility, knowledge,
definition of freedom,
They are our stage for us to exhibit who we are
They have given clarity to us as people, not just
as their parents or as couples, but as
individuals.

I am all of them
They ain't all of me
It isn't like mother like daughter
It is like daughter like mother

Time for the real flight to take off on the runway
they carved themselves over 18 years with our
struggles as three path maker and torch bearer,
They pilot their flight
They navigate their journey
And they do it with exuberance of grace,
elegance, thought, intellectual authenticity.

You came from us
And you sketched a niche for us in our existence

From Dora to Doraemon to Harry Styles to
Taylor Swift to Mass Media to Performing Arts
to Journalism to Medicine

You juggled with immaculate ease

And we stood by watching
And we stand here watching

Fly away, for
the skies await your spread, your sparkle,
The skies await you

Need we say we love you
You are our reason for us to soar

Be the reason for the world like you have always
been.

She ...The most powerful creation

Absolutely, flawlessly, breathtakingly

She is the most wonderful creation

Phir bhee,
Yugon se,
Peedee dar peedee,
Pushton se,
Use kabhee kabhee,
Kuch palon ke liye,
Kisee aate jaate lamhe pe,
Yeh jata dete hain,
Ki woh hai,
Han,
Bas itna hee,
Ki woh hai.

Only that she is there,
She is told, she is seen,
Felt and heard as per requirement though,
But, that she is indispensable to all existence,
That to all existence..... Scientific or
mythological,
She is indispensable,
That, she is indispensable and indispensable to
the core,
That all, as in all would cease to exist without
her,
This may have been researched, written, read,
And this has for sure carved a niche for the fact
that it is in the annals of history,
Irrespective has not been registered,
Thus reminders of sorts every now and then
...are given to her.

Phir bhee,
Uskee befhikree dekho,
Kaisee khamoshee se hawaion ko choo ke
guzartee hai,
Phoolon ke darmaiyan aisee shokhiyon ke saath
ghul see jaatee hai,
Raaste na dikhain,
To raaste bana letee hai,
Muskurahaton ko samet samet,
Fizaon main ghol detee hai,

*Har seher ko ek nayee subhe kee umeedon se
saja detee hai,
Har subah ko sunharee see seher ka sapna bana
detee hai,
Kaisee befhikree se chalee jaa rahee hai.*

*What a miraculous creation of the Gods,
Even the skies bow to her BEING,
For it is her BEING that gave the GODS their
BEING.*

*Apne har sajde main woh tumko dhoondhtee hai,
Uskee har dua main tumhara naam hai,
Uskee parchayee tumhara aks hai,
Aur is baat se tum vabasata na sahee,
Uske leeye to yeh sach nahee, uske wajood kee
takreer hai.*

*She doesn't complain,
No she doesn't,
She doesn't for sure,
And when you do,
She doesn't even then.*

*The one thing she carries,
With utmost humility,
The one thing that holds onto her,
The one thing that is courage for her,
The one thing that makes her hold onto you,*

That one thing,
Is her PRIDE.

Uske is guroor ko mat choona,
Uske is guroor ko mat jhuthlana,
Uske is guroor ko kabhee chunotee mat dena,
Is kader use tagaful na karna kabhee,
Woh apnee pakeezgee main khuda kee ibadat kee
meher rakhtee hai.

And if her PRIDE is challenged,
With silence as her weapon,
And silence as her shield,
She always has and always will strike back with
silence and yet, VICTORIOUS.

Uskee befhikree se aaj phir mulakat huee,
Uskee khamosh befhikree,
Uskee befhikree jo kisee waqt,
Kisee lamhe,
Kisee khithb,
Kisee Jumle,
Kisee pehchan kee mohtaj nahee hai.

Uskee befhikree jo taqdeeron kee dharohar hai.

Ritu

Jo Ruth Gayee Woh Raat Thee

Jo ruth gayee woh raat thee
Jo choot gayee woh baat thee
Rishtey kabhee ruthte nahee
Rishtey kabhee chootte nahee
Rishtey insano se hote hain
Rishton se insaan nahee hote
Naslen aur virasat insaano ko jod nahee saktee
Khoon ka rishta to ek jumla hai
Sahee mayene main to
Dil se hee dil ki rah hotee hai
Apnee parchahee ko un chehron main mat
dhoondh jo kisee wajah se tujhse jude hain
Eh bande kuda ke
Apnee parchahee ko un chehron main dhoondh
jo bewajah tujhse jude hain

Rishton ko khoon ke dayre se azad karke dekh
Rishton ko apnee takdeer maan kar mat nibha
Panee aur tamanayon kee taseer hotee hai
Rishton ko taaseer main maat dhoondh
Rishtey sirf dil kee ek halkee see dastak ke
intezar main hote hain
Us dastak ko nazarandaz mat kar
Kyunkee is dastak kee taaseer hotee hai aage
badte jana aur phir usee darwaze pe wapas na
aana
Mohabbat aur rishton ko alfazon kee bediyon
mein na bandh
Inkee paribhasha maat dhoondh
Sirf dil kee zubaan ko inhe samjhane de
Safar kuch sambhal jayega
Zindagi thodi asaan lagegee
Jise tu apna kehta hai
Jane woh kiska hai
Rishtey saboot nahee mangte
Na hee rishtey saboot dete hain
Rishtey to rishtey hote hain
Har pal ek naya bandhan
Har pal ek nayee takreer
Taaseer mat naap
Taaseer mat soch
Rait kee tarhe hath se pal nikal jayega
Kitne pal dhoondega
Kitne pal payega

Jis pal kee tune tamanna kee hai use hee toh
sapna kahte hain
Chal milen sach se
Neend mein mil lena sapne se

Zindagee mein pal ka intezar fizool hai
Har pal mein zindagee bina dhoondhe miltee hai
Tune kabhee pehchana hee nahee

Aaa jee lein zara ....

Bas Theher Ja Zara

Tareekon se bandhee hoon main,
Agaz hoon taqdeeron ka,
Mazee hoon takreeron ka.

Ek din,
Aasman ka ek tukda mujhse bola,
Meree chhaon tale ayee nahee tu kabse...kiska
intezar hai tujhe.....

Ek din,
Sooraj kee ek kiran mujhse bolee,
Kayee din hue,
Meree tapat mein tune apne ko nihara nahee
....kiska intezar hai tujhe ...

Phir ek din,
Sawan bola mujhse,
Pathjad ho chalee,
Tu mujhme bhigee nahee is baras,
Kiske intezar mein thee ....

Ek din,
Chandni bolee mujhse,
Kahan reh jaatee hai tu roz roz,
Main bikhree hotee hoon tere angan main raat
dhalte,
Kiske intezaar main rehtee hai tu in dino......

Aur phir ek din,
Zindagi bolee mujhse......
In tareekon mein,
In takreeron mein,
In taqdeeron mein.....

Is bandhan mein,
Is agaz mein,
Is mazee mein,

Tu shayad mujhe hee dhoodh rahee hai,
Main inme nahee bastee nadan,
Main to har guzarte pal mein hoon....

Theher ja zara,
Main phir mil jaungee tujhe..

Aasman ka woh tukda,
Suraj kee woh kiran,
Sawan ka bheega mausam,
Chandni ka sparsh,
In sab ko tera intezar aaj bhee hai ....
Bas theher ja zara 💕💕💕💕💕💕💕💕

Ritu

Labels

Labels never could define me,

I am all of these all the time,

Ambitious, prude, feminist, slut,

And all in one day,

And I don't shy away from any of these.

People say,

I am a wonder woman,

Yet, invisible

But, on some days,

I am not.

It is professed and preached that we be tough,

But I have come to realize,

More than being tough,

Learning how to accept vulnerabilities,

Is more important.

Every now and then

My soul runs away to a far off land,

Today I got the answer,

Why my soul takes off on these marathons,

And the answer,

To run away from myself.

We don't get stuck in the past,

Because we don't want to move on,

We get stuck in the past,

Just because it is familiar,

And also because,

We are scared of a yesterday,

So we start living for yet another yesterday.

Destiny may decide,

When and where,

Friendship strikes,

But in every insensible friendship,

Serendipity plays its role well,

And,

There it finds a sensible edifice,

Because,

As the universe fights for souls to be together,

Some of such mash ups are so strong,

THEY can't be called a coincidence,

THEY are definitely serendipity

When we let things simmer for too long,

An explosion is bound to happen,

Emotionally, physically, metaphysically,

So before we let go,

And before we move on,

A word in edgewise………

Let the dams open,

And let the simmer become serenity.

For, living on the edge,

Is as important as being indomitable,

So, every once in a while,

Why not we swipe roles,

Live on the edge,

And, see for ourselves,

The reality beyond the edge.

The ME in ME lives on

Never wanted to be,
One of those women,
Who stay silent and pretty,
On the arm of their husband,
Or
Remote and alone in the kitchen,
Doing the washing-up for that matter.

One's life must matter,
Beyond all the cooking and the cleaning and the
children,
One's life must mean more than that.

And so I have always believed,
And believe that, this day,

And, thus, I have tried my best all these years,
To nurture and breed myself,
Into being ME,
Rather than just her.

Her,
As in a denominator,
With reference,
To Her relationships.

And,
I passed on some days,
I failed on most of the days,
Today, this day, this moment included,
In every bit of what I have lived,
And live,
I pass and fail in being ME,
The ME I so nurtured and bred into being,
The ME,
I so want to be always.

Guess,
That is what is called,
A journey.

A journey,
Withered by storms,
A journey,

Where the boat hits emotions and balances back
to stability with some sane emotions.

A journey,
Where tears and fears and years and smiles,
All play a perfect fit in role plays,
Each day, one of the four being in the lead,
And on some days,
Neither of the four,
Can do nothing about anything in letting ME be.

This isn't about the victory of self over the
relationships,
This isn't about self being sublimed by
relationships,
This is about perspectives.

Simply,
Purely,
Starkly,
About perspectives.

Perspectives,
To which,
The ME,
I breed and nurture in ME,
In my being,
Each moment,
Has a right,

And thus the ME,
Survives,
In vibrance on some days as the world sees ME,
In subtle on some days as the world sees me,
The ME in ME,
Lives on

Ritu

Random is Life

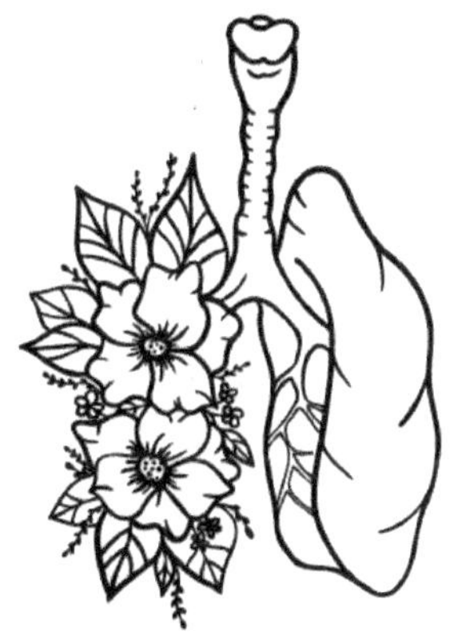

Spend a lifetime to make the shadow be your
reflection,
Stand in sunshine and see,
The shadow comes with us,
The shadow is taller, larger than life,
We walk, we move,
The shadow moves ahead of us,
Though just a shadow,
But still making the path for us.

And then we see those,
Who we will be the shadow to,
Will we be their shadow,
When our own comprehension of the shadow
that leads us is blurred,
Is sublimed by our so-called,
I AM,
how, then,
Will we be the shadow when the clock ticks,
The tong clings,
And soon it will be our turn.

Why not then,
Get a hold of our being,
And
Accept,
That by holding their hand,
Walking a bit with them,
Giving them reminders to the gaps of memory,

Filling in the blanks to their thoughts,
They still are the shadow,
Making the path.

Or else,
We will be denied by the sunshine,
The glory,
The charm,
The joy,
Of being the shadow

Woh Daro Diwar

Woh daro diwar,
Jiskee aad ko apna sa bana liya tha humne,
Woh darwaze jo doston kee ahat se khud hee
khul jaya karte the,
Woh galiyan jinse guzarte hum roz.

Woh chotee chotee baatein,
Aaj sooraj kee roshnee khuch madhyam thee
kya,
Aaj chand mere ghar ke pheeche se nikla ki
tumharee chat kee ot main chup gaya,
Tum royee thee kya aaj,
Awaz kyun bharee see hai dost,
Kuch ruth see gayee hai mehfil shayad aaj,
Chalo mana lete hain sabko,
Chalo hans lete hain,

Chalo yun hee bewajah hansa lete hain sabko,
Mahfil ko phir yaron se sajo lete hain,
Woh chotee chotee baatein.

Woh dard jo humne diye,
Bichadte milte,
Milte milate,
Woh dard jo humein ashqon se bhigo gaye,
Milte bichadte,
Milte milate.

Har pal jisme tum bhee the,
Jisme hum bhee the,
Jisme tum hum saath chale the.

Har mod jispe,
Roz milte the,
Har baat jiska kabhee afsana banaya,
Har woh baat jise kabhee taal bhee diya,
Har mulakat jo bas gayee dil mein,
Har mulakat jo tarsa detee hai aaj bhee.

Rishte jo jud gaye,
Rishte jo choot gaye,
Kitnee rahein yaad aatee hain,
Kitnee baatein yaad aatee hain,
Daro dwar,
Tum hum,
Kisse chote chote,

Baatein itnee see,
Halkee see muskurahat,
Khusheeyan jo bikheree theen,
Khusheeyan jo rooth gayee,
Khusheeyan jo chod aye,
Main aur tum hum the,
Lekin aaj,
Yeh main akela hua hai, aur dard bhee de jata
hai,

Kya itna aasan hai,
Har baar,
Har mod pe,
Rahain jab badaltee hain,
Dost jab chootte hain,
Kahanee jab adhooree see lagtee hai,
Bas bhool jana,
Bas main banke reh jana,
Bas main banke jee pana.

Sawalon kee bhool bhoolaiya hai,
Ek ankahee see kashish se,
Ek adhee adhooree see koshish bhee kartee hoon
roz,
Shayad ek din,
Khud ko in sab se alag kar loongee,
Shayad ek din samajh sakoongee,
Bhool ke age kaise nikal lete hain log,

Is waqt,
Aaj,
Abhee,
Thoda sa mushkil hai,
Dard abhee taza hai,
Chot abhee tazee hai,
Abhee pooree tarah se bichad nahee payee
hoon,

Kuch der aur,
Ae dost,
Mujhe samet ke rakh le,
Khuch pal aur,
Ae dost mere afsane rehne de fizaon mein,
Bas kuch der aur,
Bas kuch pal aur ....

Tumharee Main
Aapkee Ritu

Yet Again ... It is a New Year

At midnight yet another chapter of milestones,
enveloped with smiles, joys, battles, whims,
fantasies, warmth, affections, friendships, love,
relationships will unfold in our lives yet again

And each one of us in our own miraculous way
will welcome this new chapter.

Miraculous,
because,
each one of us truly is a miracle,
As long as we remember and understand time is
not here to stay,

Years will keep passing by,
what stays,
what gets embedded in our memories,

what starkly leaves with us a dash of sparkle
are,
relationships, love, friendships, battles won and
lost,
And a subtle closet to hold onto these memories
deeply with open arms.

And sometime,
somewhere,
someday,
when we all are gone different ways, these will
create that moment,
That moment of,
complete, absolute, pure, serene joy in our lives.

So let's each year,
As the chapter unfolds into a new page,
Let's welcome yet another journey just being
who we are,
with love, affections, warmth, forgiveness,
smiles and hugs,
To all those who make each bit of the passing
year a deeply engraved memory in our soul

Bless Be
Happy New Beginnings,
Memories cherished
Is a lot of joy.

Ego or the Pinch

Was it ego
or
Was it the pinch

It isn't always about ego,
It is the pinch most of the time.

Simplicity gets attacked blissfully most of the
time,
Acceptance gets attacked almost always,

Importantly, dependency for identity is the cue
that doesn't just get attacked,
Kills ....

How about that one person who sources your
life,
Organizes, plans, declutters your nest,
Makes you feel he or she is dependent,
When in the true sense you are.

It could be anyone,
Irrespective of gender or age
It could be your housekeeper too,
When she or he disappears and you run from
pillar to post running errands,
At times lose your job,
At times get caught in your own chaos,
At times loose relationships because your tongue
slips to harsh words,
Unknowingly, of course,
Because this source,
The housekeeper,
Way less educated,
As they say,
Not of your class either,
Not trustworthy,
Needs to be monitored,
But when it disappears from your life,
Even for a bit,
You call that his or her ego,
Forgetting it could have been a pinch of some
sort you gave,
Or agony of some sort that happened.

It's a one-sided story,
Heard, decided, sketched,
The word ego carves a niche in your life like a
stone embedded forever,
And you spill the word out,
You are done,
Anger spit out,
As the source is back,
You find yourself out of the chaos

Someone who depends on you for anything and
everything,
Give it a thought,
You depend on him or her for more than
everything.

You are not doing any favor to even those who
are dependent,
Because you are more so on them,
The word ego
Three letters
Easy to discard all the rest of the explanations,
The hurt, the pinch, the moment,
Did you indulge before passing the verdict,
Your verdict, any which way,
Simple to spell
A three letter word
EGO.

So,
Next time,
Wait,
Listen,
Understand,
No one storms into an action of appearance or
disappearance,
Without the cause and affect theory.

You were only doing yet another favor for the
dependent,
You forget that the dependent is the source of
your existence in who you are in your space.

Please,
Tread carefully,
It is rarely ego,
It is the pinch mostly.

ME

The Closed Door

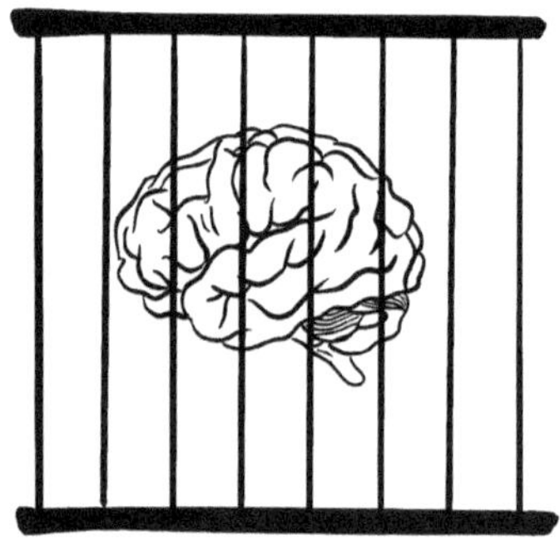

Is it really the closed door,
As put to fact,
As penned on paper,
As spoken with the belief of
"I know it all,"

This closed door,
Makes us believe,
The road ends here,
There is no rewind,

And we believe this as told,
We sit down,
Let be,
And look for some way off,

The way off,

Which will take us away from our dreams,
In fact, we might,
Might, just stop dreaming,
We do sleep,
But yet not sleep,
The fear of dreaming, yet again,
Of what we have in store behind those closed
doors,
Fear factor takes the front.

In reality, though,
There is no closed door anywhere.

No door closes on its own,
A word in edgewise,
No one can close our doors without our consent,
It is the verbal dilemma,
That entangles us so gravely,
So, so convincingly,
That closed doors,
Become reality,
And we change paths,
We give up,
We let be,
We agree that this was not meant to be for me.

Like there are no closed doors,
There are no open doors.

One door closes
The other opens,
Really,
And we believe this,
Is it life,
Or a magic show.

It is life,
The door closes,
We did not try opening it,
And dreams sealed,
Visions fractured, broke, scared.

The door opens,
We opened it,
We walked up to the door,
Pulled or pushed,
And it opened,
And there,
We could see,
The path was all lit up,
And dreams were so close,
The vision was like a crystal .

Realization seeps in,
The verbal dilemma,
Is decimated,
As we see,
What they say

Is not
Can't be,
Disappears without thunder
What we will do,
Will sparkle.

Let them say,
Let's do,
Close doors as we like,
Open doors and believe the door never closes
till we don't close.

For it is not a closet of memories,
It is a cage to our vision.

The Closed Door.

The other side

How we never see, hear and accept,
The other side,
Of life,
The other side of,
Stories,
The other side of
People,
The other side of,
Relationships.

The other side,
Most definitely,
Shifts us out of our comfort zones,
A bit so,
But it does.

The other side,

Is what Reality Bites
The other side is,
On a far away land,
In a mush of who, what,
Everything we do,
We say, is all about…

The other side,
Isn't soothing always,
Not serenity for sure,
But reality for sure,
And bites us for sure.

I am taking a trip to this other side,
Loads of lost and broken bridges,
To find and mind,
Lots of wavered off relationships,
To reach out to,
Lots of stories to listen to as real.

I am taking this trip,
To the other side,
Will be back,
And pray,
I am a better person,
Less of me,
And,
More of the zone of reality.

I saw her Today

I saw her today,
Uff! Uff! Uff!
Gorgeous to the hilt,
Emotional beyond expressions.

She was sitting in a corner,
I could hear her weeping softly,
I asked her,
What makes her weep?

She turned back to me,
Was about to say,
You won't know,
As she saw me, something stopped her,
After all, we were of the same lineage.

And then she started with her bantering,
About how beautiful the day had been,
Roses, gifts, surprises from her man,
Celebrations at work ,
A dinner date was awaiting her.

Zapped,
I again asked her,
Why do you weep,
Make much of the sprinkles of love.

She said,
"I weep because,
In a few hours 8th March will be gone,
And then 364 days,
Till she is to be the queen again,"
She went on
"kash main waqt ko rok paatee ,
I would want it to be 8th March everyday."

That is when I told her
"Woman
Celebrate yourself everyday,
Take off to those mushy lands,
Called Peace,
Every time you feel like,
Don't wait for the dates,
They are eyewash,
They are the calendar,

They are like a tick on some duty chart."

Bol to maine diya ,
But,
on second thoughts, why,
Why,
As women, we give way to these dates,
With expectations galore,
And put them to rest,
For the rest of those numbers on the calendar,
We do it,
Each one of us,
In our own ways.

Stop,
And so will the world,
Make them realize so.

Walk like a queen everyday,
You are the only creation of God who creates,
Walk with that divine bliss in your eyes,
Walk with that strength in your soul.
Walk like a woman,
Why want to be a man,
Don't carry the burden of feminism,
And,
There you go,
The day will only begin,
Never end.

WE THE ARMY WIVES

We fight,
We debate
We discuss,
We have differences of opinions,
But we still humbly submit to the bond which ties
us together.
We win, only when someone amongst us loses,
Yet, we become inspiration for the loss and
celebrate the victory,
We cry together, because we are the tears, we
smile together, because we are the smiles.
We are normal, We have dreams and desires,
We spill the milk and we cry over it,
We regret, we rejoice, we are ordinary people,
Our sacrifices don't become folklore.
Irrespective of generations we have not let any
reason be big enough to destroy our lineage.
From voice to voice
From shoulder to shoulder

From memories to memories
From Me to Her to Them
We are one soul's voice
And one soul's vision
We are the Army Wives.
The journey continues. This saga has no end.

NOT JUST BEING BUT DOING

To realize gratitude is life,
To realize smiles work like magic,
To realize blessings are miracles,
To realize showing your wounds helps them heal,
To realize showing your smiles helps them
multiply,
To realize happiness is just a perspective,
To realize you have in you the power to change
the definition of your attitude,
To realize honesty has infinite miles to go,
To realize the only truth is YOU

So BE and not DO
DON'T BE A HUMAN DOING,
BE A HUMAN BEING

TINY BEAUTIFUL THINGS

Tiny beautiful things,
Unprisoned,
By time,
Sometimes,
By emotions,
Most of the time, by
You and me.

Tiny beautiful things,
Unleashed,
Yes, unleashed,
A harsh word, though,
Because,
They lead to a roaring outpour of the soul's
agony,
But they are, irrespective
beautiful.

Tiny beautiful things,
Wouldn't allow the doors,
Of the cage to open,
If it was not family,
Family,
In the embrace of which,
These tiny little beautiful things,
Sometimes harsh,
Sometimes agonizing,
Sometimes appreciative,
Sometimes sarcastic,
Sometimes, just simply plain words,
All gripping emotions,
Ties of relationships,
Bonds of the soul,
Let the door of the cage open.

What they leave behind,
Is,
Yet another chapter,
That starts with rebonding,
And this rebonding,
Doesn't have tucks,
Stitches,
Scratches,
Knots with broken scribbles,
This rebonding is,
Yet again,

A part of,
Tiny beautiful things.

Let them simmer,
And without being through a filter of a sieve,
Let them flow.

This is all,
That life is about.
Irrespective of what the saints may prophesy
Or as lived by US as people and relationships
and friends and families

I uncage them,
These,
Tiny beautiful things,
Every now and then,
For peace deep within.

Ritu 

I AM DESTINY'S CHILD

I love the blue skies,
I love their vastness,
I love the serenity of the sun.
Screeching rays of gold glittering on my face,
And then the sunlight starts to exhaust me,
The golden rays don't soothe me anymore,
As they start piercing through my skin,
Hurting my eyes,
Burning me, tanning my soul…………………

And, just then, the dark clouds come, becoming
my veil,
Making their way through the stark blue skies,
Looking beautifully at peace,
They bring with them,
A sweet sumptuous breeze,

I crave to immerse in,
My eyes flutter for a bit,
Seeking refuge in the gentle breeze

As the clouds unleash dew drops,
I love to get drenched in the rain,
As it comes down,
It feels like heaven.

And, then, the vessel empties,
Colors play as if finding their way through a
maze,
As the dark clouds wither away,
Making way for the golden sun rays,
A new blue sky stands tall yet again,
Sheltering me, embracing me with its vastness,
Before the sunlight exhausts me,
The dark clouds are back again.

This is the way it is,
This is the way I live my life,
For, I am destiny's child, bound by destiny.

I am not the same each day,
A new victory each day, each moment,
A new failure, a new acceptance,
Denial at times, surrender with silence at times,
Roaring ...revolting ...at times,
Just being ME at times,

And, being everyone, but ME, at times……

Neither of the two,
Can be seen,
As soulfully, as beautifully,
Without each other,
Their fusion defines my existence,
For, I am destiny's child,
Bound by destiny.

The fusion is what gives me the courage,
The courage to dance to the music of victory,
That is to come tomorrow,
The fusion gives my soul a window,
A window to peep into the yesterdays,
Learning from some, refuting some and learning
from some,
The Sun and the veil of the dark cloud over the
Sun,
Is the bare truth for me,
For I am destiny's child, bound by destiny.

There is no poetry,
There is no philanthropy in these words,
These words spill life lived with reverence,
Reverence for every moment gone making way
for the next to come,
The blue skies, the golden sunshine,

Make me treasure and cherish and wait for the
rumble of the dark clouds,
And the dark clouds,
Make me treasure and cherish and wait for the
clear blue skies.
How then am I to see hope in either or neither?
There is life in all of it,
All of it is to be lived with completeness by me,
For I am destiny's child, bound by destiny.